Birds
of
NORTHEAST
OREGON

**An annotated Checklist for
Union and Wallowa
Counties**

**A
Grande Ronde Bird Club —
Oregon Dep't. of Fish & Wildlife
Publication**

**Illustrations by
Joe Evanich**

INTRODUCTION

The purpose of this checklist is two-fold: (1) to serve as a general guide to the birds that occur in Union and Wallowa Counties, and (2) to provide knowledge on the occurrence and distribution of birds in northeastern Oregon, which has been essentially neglected.

This checklist includes 50 families of birds represented by 269 species that have been reported from Union and/or Wallowa Counties since 1970. (The exception is the sharp-tailed grouse, now considered extirpated in Oregon.) Of these, 219 are considered regular breeders or visitors in one or both counties.

Nomenclature and arrangement of families and orders follow the American Ornithologists Union's (A.O.U.) 1957 Checklist of North American Birds and its supplements. All species are native unless otherwise indicated. Status and abundance of birds are based on published records in American Birds and the Grande Ronde Bird Club's newsletter, the Rav-on; information from the Oregon Department of Fish and Wildlife; and personal communications with local observers and biologists.

THE AREA

Union and Wallowa Counties occupy the northeastern corner of Oregon and are dominated by contrasting rugged mountains and vast open grassland areas. Elevations range from 9,839 feet, on Sacajawea Peak in the Wallowa Mountains, to 865 feet, along the Snake River in northern Wallowa County.

For a good example of northeastern Oregon's birdlife, a visitor should make two trips:

one during the summer and one during the winter. Although July and August temperatures reach the nineties and low hundreds, the summers are dry and pleasant. Campgrounds are numerous and generally uncrowded. The Eagle Cap Wilderness Area is especially attractive to backpackers. The summer mountain birds include flammulated and saw-whet owls, spruce and blue grouse, various woodpeckers, northern goshawks, and prairie falcons.

January temperatures, however, drop to well below freezing. Snow is encountered during this time of year, but the main highways are usually kept open. During the winter, such northern species as Bohemian Waxwings and tree sparrows are common fare, and many of these birds are rarely seen elsewhere in Oregon.

Habitats vary from alpine in the Wallowa Mountains, through mixed conifer forests (dispersed with grasslands), to open grasslands and sagebrush flats. The Grande Ronde Valley, which was once a vast marshy river basin, and the Wallowa Valley are intensively farmed. Ladd Marsh Wildlife Management Area, south of La Grande, is the only large remnant of marsh habitat left in the Grande Ronde Valley. Scattered cottonwoods and willows occur along the valley waterways as well as some dense patches of riparian shrubs. There are a few open bodies of water. Migrant waterfowl congregate on Wallowa Lake, Wallowa Fish Hatchery ponds, and the Joseph sewage ponds in Wallowa County; and the confluence of Ladd and Catherine Creeks, Conley and Morgan Lakes and the La Grande sewage ponds in Union County. During wet springs and falls, waterfowl and migrant shorebirds are also seen in many of the flooded fields.

A NOTE OF CAUTION:

We urge you to be cautious so that others may also enjoy the same sights and sounds you are experiencing.

Remember that you are a visitor peering into the birds' community, and if you pass over some invisible threshold, you become an intruder.

Some birds require specific areas for courtship, such as the sage grouse lek. Unnecessary or continued disturbance may reduce their productivity because their courtship behavior has been interrupted once too often.

No nest sites should be disturbed, even for a peek at the eggs or young. In some cases your activities may cause the parents to abandon the nest, and more often, you leave the evidence a predator needs to find his next meal.

KEY TO THE CHECKLIST

Nomenclature used in this checklist follows that found in the American Ornithologists Union's Checklist of North American Brids, Fifth Edition (1957) and its supplements. All species are native unless otherwise indicated.

The following symbols and terms are used in the checklist:

Abundant--can be found in good numbers (> 20) on almost all trips.

Common--a few (< 20) found on almost all trips.

Uncommon--a few (< 20) found on only a few trips.

Occasional--very small numbers (< 10) found on a few trips almost every year.

Rare--very small numbers (< 10) found on very few trips, seldom every year.

Accidental--out of normal range and fewer than five records for the two-county region.

Hypothetical--an unconfirmed occurrence; to be confirmed, a sighting must be supported by a specimen, an identifiable photograph, or at least two observers.

The above status terms are applicable only in proper habitat and during appropriate season.

*--breeds in two-county area.
U--recorded in Union County only.
W--recorded in Wallowa County only.

Seasons:

    Spring--March 1-May 31
    Summer--June 1-July 31
    Fall--August 1-October 31
    Winter--November 1-February 28(29)

Elevation:

    Low--850-3500 ft.
    Moderate--3500-6000 ft.
    High--6000 and up

ORDER GAVIIFORMES

FAMILY GAVIIDAE

COMMON LOON (Gavia immer)

Uncommon spring and fall migrant, occasional winter resident. Restricted to lakes and other large bodies of water at low to moderate elevations; most common on Wallowa Lake, Wallowa County.

ORDER PODICIPEDIFORMES

FAMILY PODICIPEDIDAE

RED-NECKED GREBE (Podiceps grisegena)   W

Rare spring and fall migrant on large open bodies of water at low elevations; most records are from Wallowa Lake, Wallowa County.

HORNED GREBE* (Podiceps auritus)

Occasional spring and fall migrant, rare summer and winter resident; has nested on Downy Lake, Wallowa County. Usually found at low elevations on open bodies of water during migration, marshy areas for nesting.

EARED GREBE* (Podiceps nigricollis)

Uncommon spring and fall migrant, occasional summer resident; breeds locally. Habitat preference similar to Horned Grebe's.

WESTERN GREBE (Aechmophorus occidentalis)

Uncommon spring and fall migrant and summer visitor. Usually found on large open bodies of water at low elevations.

PIED-BILLED GREBE* (Podilymbus podiceps)

Uncommon spring and fall migrant and summer resident, occasional winter resident at low elevations. Breeds on marshes, ponds, small lakes; migrates and winters on large bodies of water.

ORDER PELECANIFORMES

FAMILY PELECANIDAE

WHITE PELICAN (Pelecanus erythrorhynchos)

Rare spring and fall migrant on large bodies of water in Grande Ronde and Wallowa River Valleys at low elevations.

FAMILY PHALACROCORACIDAE

DOUBLE-CRESTED CORMORANT (Phalacrocorax auritus)

Occasional spring and fall migrant near water in Grande Ronde and Wallowa River Valleys at low elevations.

ORDER CICONIIFORMES

FAMILY ARDEIDAE

GREAT BLUE HERON* (Ardea herodias)

Common resident in wetland areas at low to moderate elevations; some withdrawal from northeastern Oregon during winter. Major rookeries are in Grande Ronde and Wallowa River drainages.

GREEN HERON (<u>Butorides</u> <u>striatus</u>)   U

Accidental, one record: one bird observed in Grande Ronde Valley near La Grande, Union County on 26 May 1979. Three observers.

GREAT EGRET (<u>Casmerodias</u> <u>albus</u>)   U

Rare summer visitor in low elevation wetlands of Grande Ronde Valley; most records are during June.

SNOWY EGRET (<u>Egretta</u> <u>thula</u>)   W

Hypothetical, one record: one bird observed at Wallowa Fish Hatchery near Enterprise, Wallowa County on 4 June 1980. One observer.

BLACK-CROWNED NIGHT HERON* (<u>Nycticorax</u> <u>nycticorax</u>)

Uncommon spring and fall migrant and summer resident, no winter records. Prefers marsh and swamp land at low elevations.

AMERICAN BITTERN* (<u>Botaurus</u> <u>lentiginosus</u>)

Uncommon spring and fall migrant and summer resident, no winter records. Found in dense cattail and tule marshes of Grande Ronde and Wallowa River Valleys; much less common in Wallowa County.

FAMILY THRESKIORNITHIDAE

WHITE-FACED IBIS (<u>Plegadis</u> <u>chihi</u>)   U

Accidental, one record: three birds found in Grande Ronde Valley near Hot Lake, Union County during May 1977. Photographed.

—Barrow's Goldeneye—

ORDER ANSERIFORMES

FAMILY ANATIDAE

WHISTLING SWAN (Olor columbianus)

Common spring and fall migrant, uncommon winter resident. Found on large bodies of water in Grande Ronde and Wallowa Valleys at low to moderate elevations.

TRUMPETER SWAN (Olor buccinator)   W

Rare spring and fall migrant and winter visitor to large bodies of water in Grande Ronde and Wallowa Valleys at low to moderate elevations.

CANADA GOOSE* (Branta canadensis)

Abundant spring and fall migrant, common summer resident, uncommon winter resident. Found in wetlands and crop fields of most valleys at low to moderate elevations.

WHITE-FRONTED GOOSE (Anser albifrons)

Common spring and uncommon fall migrant in wetlands and crop fields of Grande Ronde and Wallowa Valleys at low elevations.

SNOW GOOSE (Chen caerulescens)

Uncommon spring and fall migrant through wetlands and cropfields of Grande Ronde and Wallowa Valleys at low elevations.

MALLARD* (Anas platyrhynchos)

Abundant spring and fall migrant, common summer and winter resident. Found on marshes, ponds, lakes, sloughs, almost any body of water at low to high elevations.

GADWALL* (Anas strepera)

Common spring and fall migrant, uncommon summer resident, occasional winter resident. Found in ponds, lakes, marshes, at lower elevations.

AMERICAN PINTAIL* (Anas acuta)

Abundant spring and fall migrant, common summer resident, uncommon winter resident. Found on ponds, lakes, marshes, usually at lower elevations.

GREEN-WINGED TEAL* (Anas crecca)

Uncommon spring and fall migrant, occasional summer and winter resident. Found on lakes, marshes, flooded fields, etc. at lower elevations.

BLUE-WINGED TEAL* (Anas discors)

Common spring and fall migrant, uncommon summer resident, no winter records. Habitat preference similar to Green-Winged Teal's.

CINNAMON TEAL* (Anas cyanoptera)

Abundant spring and fall migrant, common summer

resident, no winter records. Habitat preference similar to Green-Winged Teal's.

EUROPEAN WIGEON (Anas penelope)   U

Accidental, one verified record: five birds seen in Grande Ronde Valley near La Grande, Union County on 26 March 1977. Four observers.

AMERICAN WIGEON* (Anas americana)

Common spring and fall migrant, uncommon summer resident, occasional winter resident. Usually found on lakes, ponds, flooded fields, etc. at low elevations.

NORTHERN SHOVELER* (Anas clypeata)

Common spring and fall migrant, uncommon summer resident, no winter records. Found on lakes, ponds, sloughs, etc. at low elevations.

WOOD DUCK* (Aix sponsa)

Uncommon spring and fall migrant, uncommon summer resident, rare winter resident. Prefers wooded marshes, small ponds, lakes at low elevations.

REDHEAD* (Aythya americana)

Common spring and fall migrant, uncommon summer resident, occasional winter resident. Found on lakes, larger ponds, sloughs, etc. at low elevations.

CANVASBACK* (Aythya valisineria)

Uncommon spring and fall migrant, occasional summer and winter resident; breeds locally. Found on larger bodies of water, large ponds in Grande Ronde and Wallowa Valleys at low elevations.

RING-NECKED DUCK* (Aythya collaris)

Uncommon spring and fall migrant and summer resident, occasional winter resident. Habitat preference similar to Redhead's, but breeds on wooded lakes and ponds.

LESSER SCAUP (Aythya affinis)

Uncommon spring and fall migrant, occasional summer resident, rare winter resident. Habitat preference similar to Redhead's.

COMMON GOLDENEYE (Bucephala clangula)

Common spring and fall migrant and winter visitor, rare summer visitor. Prefers larger deeper ponds and lakes at low to moderate elevations.

BARROW'S GOLDENEYE (Bucephala islandica)

Uncommon spring and fall migrant and winter visitor. Habitat preference similar to Common Goldeneye's.

BUFFLEHEAD (Bucephala albeola)

Common spring and fall migrant, uncommon winter resident. Habitat preference similar to Common Goldeneye's.

HARLEQUIN DUCK (Histrionicus histrionicus)   W

Rare summer resident on swift streams at moderate to high elevations in the Wallowa and Blue Mountains. Probably breeds; last nesting record 1935.

RUDDY DUCK* (<u>Oxyura jamaicensis</u>)

Uncommon spring and fall migrant and summer resident, rare winter resident. Found on larger bodies of water during migration, breeds on marshy ponds and lakes at low elevations.

HOODED MERGANSER (<u>Lophodytes cucullatus</u>)

Occasional to uncommon during spring and fall migration, occasional summer resident, uncommon winter resident. Generally found in marshes or wooded bodies of water at low elevations.

COMMON MERGANSER* (<u>Mergus merganser</u>)

Common spring and fall migrant, uncommon summer and winter resident. Prefers lakes, large ponds, rivers, at low to moderate elevations.

ORDER FALCONIFORMES

FAMILY CATHARTIDAE

TURKEY VULTURE* (<u>Cathartes aura</u>)

Uncommon spring and fall migrant, common summer resident. Usually seen over open country at low to high elevations. Breeds locally.

—Swainson's Hawk—

FAMILY ACCIPITRIDAE

NORTHERN GOSHAWK* (_Accipiter_ _gentilis_)

Uncommon resident, breeding in heavily forested areas of moderate to high elevations. Many move to open country at lower elevations during winter.

SHARP-SHINNED HAWK* (_Accipiter_ _striatus_)

Uncommon resident, found in coniferous forest at moderate to high elevations, but often winters at lower elevations in open and deciduous country.

COOPER'S HAWK* (_Accipiter_ _cooperii_)

Uncommon resident. Habitat preference similar to Sharp-Shinned Hawk's.

RED-TAILED HAWK* (_Buteo_ _jamaicensis_)

Common resident in open land and light forest, mostly at low to moderate elevations.

SWAINSON'S HAWK* (Buteo swainsoni)

Uncommon spring and fall migrant and summer resident, no winter records. Found in valleys and rolling grasslands at low elevations; more common during migration.

ROUGH-LEGGED HAWK (Buteo lagopus)

Common winter visitor in open country at low to moderate elevations.

FERRUGINOUS HAWK* (Buteo regalis)

Occasional (locally common) summer resident, rare winter resident. Prefers grassland and sagebrush areas at low to moderate elevations; most common in Zumwalt region of Wallowa County.

GOLDEN EAGLE* (Aquila chrysaetos)

Uncommon resident in open country at low to high elevations, less common in forested regions; prefers rimrock.

BALD EAGLE (Haliaeetus leucocephalus)

Occasional to uncommon winter visitor, rare summer resident; possibly nests. Prefers open country or broken woodland at low to moderate elevations.

MARSH HAWK (NORTHERN HARRIER)* (Circus cyaneus)

Common resident of marsh and grass areas at low to moderate elevations; less numerous during winter.

FAMILY PANDIONIDAE

OSPREY* (Pandion haliaetus)

Uncommon spring and fall migrant, occasional summer resident, breeds very locally. Prefers forested or semi-forested country always near water at low to moderate elevations.

FAMILY FALCONIDAE

PRAIRIE FALCON* (Falco mexicanus)

Uncommon resident in grassland and open woodland, especially about rimrock, at low to moderate elevations. Moves to valleys during winter.

PEREGRINE FALCON (Falco peregrinus)

Rare winter visitor to open country at low to moderate elevations.

MERLIN (Falco columbarius)

Occasional spring and fall migrant and winter visitor, usually in open or semi-wooded country at low to moderate elevations.

AMERICAN KESTREL* (Falco sparverius)

Common spring and fall migrant and summer resident, uncommon winter resident. Prefers open country and open woodland at low to moderate elevations.

— Spruce Grouse —

ORDER GALLIFORMES

FAMILY TETRAONIDAE

BLUE GROUSE* (<u>Dendragapus</u> <u>obscurus</u>)

Common but elusive resident of the Blue and Wallowa Mountains and their higher foothills. Prefers coniferous forest at moderate to high elevations; some move to lower elevations during winter.

SPRUCE GROUSE* (<u>Canachites</u> <u>canadensis</u>)

Uncommon and elusive resident of Wallowa Mountains only. Found exclusively in coniferous forest at moderate to high elevations.

RUFFED GROUSE* (<u>Bonasa</u> <u>umbellus</u>)

Uncommon to common resident of coniferous and mixed forests at low to moderate elevations. Some movement to lower elevations during winter.

WHITE-TAILED PTARMIGAN* (Lagopus leucurus)   W

Very rare resident of north-central Wallowa Mountains in Wallowa County. Introduced to northeastern Oregon in 1967; last seen in November 1980 near Bonny Lakes, Wallowa County. Strictly an alpine species.

SHARP-TAILED GROUSE (Pedioecetes phasianellus)

Probably extirpated from northeastern Oregon. Formerly found in native grassland at low to moderate elevations. Last seen in Zumwalt region of Wallowa County.

SAGE GROUSE* (Centrocercus urophasianus)   U

Occasional resident in sagebrush areas of southern Union County near North Powder and Medical Springs.

FAMILY PHASIANIDAE

COMMON BOBWHITE* (Colinus virginianus)   W

Rare resident; recently introduced (less than ten years ago) in agricultural lands around Enterprise, Wallowa County.

CALIFORNIA QUAIL* (Lophortyx californicus)

Common resident at low to moderate elevations in open country. Some movement to lower elevations during winter.

MOUNTAIN QUAIL* (Oreortyx pictus)

Occasional resident at moderate elevations in open and brushy country. Some movement to lower elevations during winter.

RING-NECKED PHEASANT* (<u>Phasianus</u> <u>colchicus</u>)

Common introduced resident at low to moderate elevations in agricultural and grassy country.

CHUKAR* (<u>Alectoris</u> <u>chukar</u>)

Common (locally abundant) introduced resident of rocky hillside country at low to moderate elevations.

GRAY PARTRIDGE* (<u>Perdix</u> <u>perdix</u>)

Common introduced resident (though elusive during summer) of farmland and grassland of Grande Ronde and Wallowa Valleys.

FAMILY MELEAGRIDIDAE

TURKEY* (<u>Meleagris</u> <u>gallopavo</u>)

Rare introduced resident of Blue Mountains in northern half of the two counties. Prefers open coniferous woodland at low to moderate elevations.

— Turkey —

—Sandhill Crane—

ORDER GRUIFORMES

FAMILY GRUIDAE

SANDHILL CRANE* (<u>Grus</u> <u>canadensis</u>) U

Occasional spring and fall migrant and summer resident; breeds locally at Ladd Marsh, Union County. Prefers marshy fields, grain fields at low elevations.

FAMILY RALLIDAE

VIRGINIA RAIL* (<u>Rallus</u> <u>limicola</u>)

Uncommon spring and fall migrant and summer resident, occasional winter resident. Found mostly in cattail and tule marshes at low elevations.

SORA* (<u>Porzana</u> <u>carolina</u>)

Common spring and fall migrant, uncommon summer resident, no winter records. Habitat preference similar to Virginia Rail's, but not as limited to marsh areas.

AMERICAN COOT* (Fulica americana)

Abundant spring and fall migrant, common summer resident, occasional winter resident. Habitat includes almost any body of water at low to moderate elevations.

ORDER CHARADRIIFORMES

FAMILY CHARADRIIDAE

SEMIPALMATED PLOVER (Charadrius semipalmatus)

Uncommon spring and occasional fall migrant to wet fields and mudflats of Grande Ronde and Wallowa Valleys at low elevations.

KILLDEER* (Charadrius vociferous)

Abundant spring and fall migrant and summer resident, uncommon winter resident. Found in open fields and pastures, often far from water, at low to moderate elevations.

FAMILY SCOLOPACIDAE

COMMON SNIPE* (Capella gallinago)

Common spring and fall migrant and summer resident, occasional winter resident. Found in wet fields, bogs, grassy margins of lakes and rivers at low to moderate elevations.

LONG-BILLED CURLEW* (Numenius americanus)

Uncommon spring and fall migrant and summer resident, no winter records. Found in pastures, fields, often far from water at low to moderate elevations.

WHIMBREL (Numenius phaeopus)   U

Accidental, one record: one bird seen with Long-Billed Curlews in Grande Ronde Valley near La Grande, Union County on 26 May 1979. Three observers.

UPLAND SANDPIPER (Bartramia longicauda)   U

Very rare summer and fall migrant in Union County. Found in meadows at moderate elevations.

SPOTTED SANDPIPER* (Actitis macularia)

Common spring and fall migrant and summer resident, no winter records. Found on gravelly or grassy margins of lakes, rivers, ponds at low to moderate elevations.

SOLITARY SANDPIPER (Tringa solitaria)

Occasional spring and fall migrant, mostly in wet fields and ponds at low to moderate elevations.

GREATER YELLOWLEGS (Tringa melanoleuca)

Uncommon spring and fall migrant in wet fields, ponds, mudflats, etc. of Grande Ronde and Wallowa Valleys at low elevations.

LESSER YELLOWLEGS (Tringa flavipes)

Uncommon spring and fall migrant in similar habitat to Greater Yellowlegs.

WILLET (Catoptrophorus semipalmatus)

Rare spring migrant in grassy fields, ponds, lake margins in Grande Ronde and Wallowa Valleys at low elevations.

WESTERN SANDPIPER (Calidris mauri)

Common spring and fall migrant in wet fields, ponds, mudflats, etc. at low to moderate elevations.

SEMIPALMATED SANDPIPER (Calidris pusilla)   U

Accidental, one record: one bird found with Western Sandpipers at Mouth of Ladd Creek, Union County on 11 August 1980. Two observers.

LEAST SANDPIPER (Calidris minutilla)

Common spring and fall migrant in wet fields, ponds, mudflats, etc. at low elevations.

BAIRD'S SANDPIPER (Calidris bairdii)

Uncommon spring and fall migrant in habitat similar to Least Sandpiper's as well as high elevation lakes and ponds.

PECTORAL SANDPIPER (Calidris melanotos)

Occasional spring and uncommon fall migrant. Habitat preference similar to Least Sandpiper's.

DUNLIN (Calidris alpina)

Rare spring and fall migrant in habitat similar to Least Sandpiper.

SANDERLING (Calidris alba)

Very rare fall migrant in habitat similar to Least Sandpiper.

LONG-BILLED DOWITCHER (<u>Limnodromus</u>
<u>scolopaceus</u>)

Uncommon spring and fall migrant in wet fields,
ponds, mudflats of Grande Ronde and Wallowa
Valleys at low elevations.

MARBLED GODWIT (<u>Limosa</u> <u>fedoa</u>)

Very rare spring and fall migrant in wet
fields, mudflats, etc. of Grande Ronde and
Wallowa Valleys at low elevations.

FAMILY RECURVIROSTRIDAE

AMERICAN AVOCET* (<u>Recurvirostra</u> <u>americana</u>)

Locally uncommon spring and fall migrant and
summer resident; rare as a nesting species.
Prefers ponds, wet fields, especially alkali
waters at low elevations.

BLACK-NECKED STILT (<u>Himantopus</u> <u>mexicanus</u>)　　U

Accidental, one record: "several" (about five)
birds were found in the Grande Ronde Valley
near La Grande, Union County on 1-13 May 1977.
Many observers present.

— Wilson's Phalarope —

FAMILY PHALAROPODIDAE

WILSON'S PHALAROPE* (<u>Steganopus</u> <u>tricolor</u>)

Locally uncommon spring and fall migrant and
summer resident; breeds very locally. Habitat
preference similar to American Avocet's.

NORTHERN PHALAROPE (<u>Lobipes</u> <u>lobatus</u>)

Occasional to uncommon spring and fall migrant
in flooded fields, ponds, shallow waters at
low elevations.

FAMILY STERCORARIIDAE

PARASITIC JAEGER (<u>Stercorarius</u> <u>parasiticus</u>)   W

Hypothetical, one record: one bird seen
harassing gulls at Wallowa Lake State Park,
Wallowa County on 9 September 1980. One
observer.

FAMILY LARIDAE

CALIFORNIA GULL (Larus californicus)

Occasional spring and fall migrant and summer visitor, rare winter resident. Prefers wet fields, lakes, ponds at low elevations.

RING-BILLED GULL (Larus delawarensis)

Uncommon spring and fall migrant and summer visitor, occasional winter visitor in similar habitat as California Gull.

MEW GULL (Larus canus)   U

Accidental, two records: one bird found dead at Alicel in the Grande Ronde Valley, Union County on 18 February 1976, specimen. A different bird picked up injured at Anthony Lakes Ski Area, Union-Baker County line on 20 February 1976; released near La Grande, Union County.

FRANKLIN'S GULL (Larus pipixcan)

Very rare spring migrant in Grande Ronde and Wallowa Valleys, usually on larger bodies of water at low elevations.

BONAPARTE'S GULL (Larus philadelphia)

Occasional to uncommon spring and fall migrant in similar habitat as Franklin's Gull.

FORSTER'S TERN (Sterna forsteri)

Rare spring migrant on lakes, large ponds, and over wet fields of Grande Ronde and Wallowa Valleys at low elevations.

CASPIAN TERN (Sterna caspia)

Occasional spring and fall migrant and summer visitor in similar habitat as Forster's Tern.

BLACK TERN (Chlidonias niger)

Occasional spring and summer migrant in marshes, wet fields, lakes at low elevations.

ORDER COLUMBIFORMES

FAMILY COLUMBIDAE

BAND-TAILED PIGEON (Columba fasciata)

Rare spring and summer migrant in wooded areas at low to moderate elevations.

ROCK DOVE (DOMESTIC PIGEON)* (Columba livia)

Abundant introduced resident around buildings and other structures in settled areas; less common in basalt cliff areas.

MOURNING DOVE* (Zenaida macroura)

Common spring and fall migrant and summer resident, uncommon winter resident. Found in open forest and agricultural areas at low to moderate elevations.

ORDER CUCULIFORMES

FAMILY CUCULIDAE

YELLOW-BILLED CUCKOO (Coccyzus americanus)

Accidental, two verified records: one bird spent a week in La Grande, Union County during the 1950's (date unrecorded); specimen. Two birds found in La Grande, Union County in August 1980; four observers.

ORDER STRIGIFORMES

FAMILY TYTONIDAE

BARN OWL* (<u>Tyto</u> <u>alba</u>)

Uncommon resident, found about old buildings in open and semi-wooded country at low to moderate elevations.

— Flammulated Owl —

FAMILY STRIGIDAE

SCREECH OWL* (<u>Otus</u> <u>asio</u>)

Uncommon resident in deciduous and mixed forest at low to moderate elevations.

FLAMMULATED OWL* (<u>Otus</u> <u>flammeolus</u>)

Locally uncommon summer resident. Found in coniferous forest (especially Ponderosa Pine) at moderate elevations in Blue and Wallowa Mountains.

GREAT HORNED OWL* (Bubo virgianus)

Common resident in all types of woodland at low to high elevations; less common in open areas such as rimrock.

SNOWY OWL (Nyctea scandiaca)

Very rare winter visitor in open country at low to moderate elevations.

NORTHERN PYGMY OWL* (Glaucidium gnoma)

Uncommon resident in coniferous and deciduous woodland at low to moderate elevations; much more conspicuous during winter.

BURROWING OWL* (Athene cunicularia)

Locally uncommon summer resident in native grassland and sagebrush areas at low to moderate elevations; rare as a breeding bird.

BARRED OWL* (Strix varia)

Rare resident found in coniferous and mixed forest areas at low to moderate elevations; first recorded in northeastern Oregon along Wenaha River, Wallowa County in May 1974.

GREAT GRAY OWL* (Strix nebulosa)

Occasional resident in coniferous forests adjacent to meadows at moderate to high elevations in the Blue and Wallowa Mountains.

LONG-EARED OWL* (Asio otus)

Occasional summer resident in coniferous or mixed forest at low to moderate elevations; no winter records.

UNION & WALLOWA COUNTIES

TO WESTON

204

BLUE MOUNT

Umatilla Co.

BLUE

Elgin
Rhineha

TO
PENDLETON

Summerville
Imbler

82

Grande

LaGrande

Ronde

Valley

244

84

TO UKIAH

BLUE

MOUNTAINS

237

North
Powder

Grant Co.

TO BAKER

● City / Town

84 Interstate

3 State Route

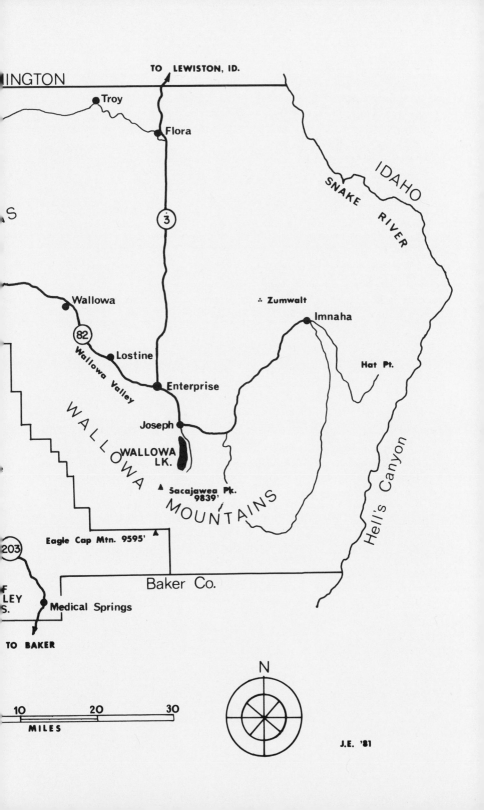

SHORT-EARED OWL* (Asio flammeus)

Uncommon to common resident in open fields, agricultural land, and marshes at low to moderate elevations.

SAW-WHET OWL* (Aegolius acadius)

Uncommon resident of coniferous forest at low to moderate elevations.

ORDER CAPRIMULGIFORMES

FAMILY CAPRIMULIGIDAE

POOR-WILL (Phalaenoptilus nuttallii)　　　U

Uncommon summer resident in sagebrush and native grassland areas with rimrock at low to moderate elevations; probably nests.

COMMON NIGHTHAWK* (Chordeiles minor)

Common spring and fall migrant and summer resident. Prefers open country; over towns, grasslands, etc. at low to moderate elevations.

ORDER APODIFORMES

FAMILY APODIDAE

BLACK SWIFT (Cypseloides niger)　　　W

Accidental, two records: one bird seen at Hat Point, Wallowa County in August 1977, one observer. Two birds seen at Summit Ridge, Wallowa County on 3 July 1979; two observers.

VAUX'S SWIFT* (Chaetura vauxi)

Common to abundant spring and fall migrant and summer resident over towns, open forest, forages over open country also; generally at low to moderate elevations.

WHITE-THROATED SWIFT* (Aeronautes saxatalis) W

Rare spring migrant and summer resident along Hell's Canyon, Wallowa County as well as other cliff regions of the Snake River; breeds locally.

FAMILY TROCHILIDAE

BLACK-CHINNED HUMMINGBIRD* (Archilochus alexandri)

Uncommon spring and fall migrant and summer resident in open woodland and towns at low to moderate elevations.

BROAD-TAILED HUMMINGBIRD (Selasphorus platycercus)

Occasional spring and fall migrant and summer resident; probably breeds. Found in meadows and open woodland at moderate to high elevations. Also migrates through towns at lower elevations.

RUFOUS HUMMINGBIRD* (Selasphorus rufus)

Uncommon spring and fall migrant and summer resident. Habitat preference similar to Black-Chinned Hummingbird's.

CALLIOPE HUMMINGBIRD* (Stellula calliope)

Uncommon spring and fall migrant and summer resident in same habitat as Broad-Tailed Hummingbird.

ORDER CORACIIFORMES

FAMILY ALCEDINIDAE

BELTED KINGFISHER* (<u>Megaceryle</u> <u>alcyon</u>)

Uncommon resident near water in open and semi-wooded country at low to moderate elevations. Less numerous during winter.

— Black-backed
Three-toed Woodpecker —

ORDER PICIFORMES

FAMILY PICIDAE

COMMON FLICKER* (<u>Colaptes</u> <u>auratus</u>)

Common resident in coniferous and deciduous forest and semi-wooded country at low to high elevations. The Red-Shafted Flicker, <u>C</u>. <u>a</u>. <u>cafer</u>, is the common subspecies here.

PILEATED WOODPECKER* (<u>Dryocopus</u> <u>pileatus</u>)

Uncommon resident in mature stands of timber; prefers coniferous woodland at low to moderate elevations.

LEWIS' WOODPECKER* (Asyndesmus lewis)

Uncommon spring and fall migrant and summer resident, occasional winter resident. Found in open woodland and riparian growth at low to moderate elevations.

YELLOW-BELLIED SAPSUCKER* (Sphyrapicus varius)

Uncommon summer resident at low to moderate elevations in open deciduous or mixed woodland; no winter records. The Red-Naped Sapsucker, S. v. nuchalis, is the common subspecies here.

WILLIAMSON'S SAPSUCKER* (Sphyrapicus thyroideus)

Uncommon summer resident, no winter records. Found in mixed coniferous forest (especially pine) of Wallowa and Blue Mountains at moderate elevations.

HAIRY WOODPECKER* (Picoides villosus)

Common resident in both coniferous and deciduous forest at low to moderate elevations.

DOWNY WOODPECKER* (Picoides pubescens)

Common resident in deciduous and mixed woodland and riparian growth at low to moderate elevations.

WHITE-HEADED WOODPECKER* (Picoides albolarvatus)

Uncommon resident of open coniferous (especially pine) forest at moderate elevations.

BLACK-BACKED THREE-TOED WOODPECKER* (Picoides arcticus)

Uncommon resident of coniferous forest, especially lodgepole pine, at moderate to high elevations.

NORTHERN THREE-TOED WOODPECKER* (Picoides tridactylus)

Uncommon resident in similar habitat as Black-Backed Three-Toed Woodpecker.

ORDER PASSERIFORMES

FAMILY TYRANNIDAE

EASTERN KINGBIRD* (Tyrannus tyrannus)

Uncommon spring and fall migrant, locally common summer resident. Found in riparian growth and open woodland at low elevations.

WESTERN KINGBIRD* (Tyrannus verticalis)

Common spring and fall migrant and summer resident in farmland, open woodland, etc., at low to moderate elevations.

ASH-THROATED FLYCATCHER (Myiarchus cinerascens)

Accidental, two records: one bird found at Rhinehart near Elgin, Union County on 26 June 1977; one observer. One bird seen near Imnaha, Wallowa County in May 1976; two observers.

SAY'S PHOEBE* (Sayornis saya)

Uncommon spring and fall migrant and summer resident. Prefers farmland, ranches, other open and usually arid areas at low elevations.

WILLOW FLYCATCHER* (Empidonax traillii)

Common spring and fall migrant and summer
resident. Found in open deciduous forest with
brushy growth and riparian areas at low
elevations.

ALDER FLYCATCHER (Empidonax alnorum)   W

Accidental, one record: one bird seen and heard
at Wallowa Fish Hatchery near Enterprise,
Wallowa County on 21 June 1980. Four
observers.

HAMMOND'S FLYCATCHER* (Empidonax hammondii)

Uncommon spring and fall migrant and summer
resident in mature coniferous forest (generally
pine, spruce, fir) at moderate to high
elevations.

DUSKY FLYCATCHER* (Empidonax oberholseri)

Uncommon spring and fall migrant and summer
resident in mixed or coniferous forest with
brushy undergrowth at moderate elevations; also
migrates at lower elevations.

WESTERN FLYCATCHER* (Empidonax difficilis)

Occasional summer resident in deciduous and
open coniferous woodland at low to moderate
elevations; has nested near Lostine, Wallowa
County.

WESTERN WOOD PEWEE* (Contopus sordidulus)

Common spring and fall migrant and summer
resident. Prefers semi-open deciduous or
coniferous woodland at low to moderate
elevations.

OLIVE-SIDED FLYCATCHER* (<u>Nuttallornis</u> <u>borealis</u>)

Uncommon to common spring and fall migrant and summer resident in open coniferous forest at low to moderate elevations.

FAMILY ALAUDIDAE

HORNED LARK* (<u>Eremophilia</u> <u>alpestris</u>)

Common to abundant spring and fall migrant and winter resident, uncommon summer resident. Found in open country, especially farmland and sagebrush areas at low to moderate elevations.

— Tree Swallow —

FAMILY HIRUNDINIDAE

VIOLET-GREEN SWALLOW* (<u>Tachycineta</u> <u>thalassina</u>)

Common to abundant spring and fall migrant, common summer resident. Found in open country about towns, farmland, open forest at low to moderate elevations.

TREE SWALLOW* (Iridoprocne bicolor)

Common summer resident. Prefers similar habitat as Violet-Green Swallow.

BANK SWALLOW* (Riparia riparia)

Locally common summer resident in isolated colonies where there are suitable nesting banks. Prefers sandy soil usually near water at low elevations.

ROUGH-WINGED SWALLOW* (Stelgidopteryx ruficollis)

Uncommon to common spring and fall migrant and summer resident in similar habitat to Bank Swallow.

BARN SWALLOW* (Hirundo rustica)

Common to abundant spring and fall migrant and summer resident in similar habitat as Violet-Green Swallow.

CLIFF SWALLOW* (Petrochelidon pyrrhonota)

Locally common spring and fall migrant and summer resident, nesting around buildings and bridges in open country at low elevations.

FAMILY CORVIDAE

GRAY JAY* (Perisoreus canadensis)

Uncommon resident in coniferous forest of Blue and Wallowa Mountains at moderate to high elevations.

BLUE JAY* (Cyanocitta cristata)

A recent rare straggler to northeastern Oregon, usually during fall and winter. Records are from Union and La Grande in Union County and Enterprise in Wallowa County, all since 1976. Has nested in Union, Union County (1977).

STELLER'S JAY* (Cyanocitta stelleri)

Common resident in coniferous or mixed forest at low to high elevations; wanders into towns and cities during winter.

SCRUB JAY (Aphelocoma coerulescens)   U

Hypothetical, one record: one bird seen in La Grande, Union County on 22 July 1980. One observer.

BLACK-BILLED MAGPIE* (Pica pica)

Common resident in open country such as farmland, sagebrush areas, etc. at low to moderate elevations.

COMMON RAVEN* (Corvus corax)

Common resident in open areas and open forest at low to high elevations.

COMMON CROW* (Corvus brachyrhynchos)

Common spring and fall migrant and summer resident, occasional winter resident. Prefers open country similar to Black-Billed Magpie, but more often found around towns.

CLARK'S NUTCRACKER* (Nucifraga columbiana)

Uncommon resident, prefers open coniferous forest at high elevations during summer; moves to lower elevations during winter.

FAMILY PARIDAE

BLACK-CAPPED CHICKADEE* (<u>Parus</u> <u>atricapillus</u>)

Common resident in deciduous woods and riparian growth at low to moderate elevations.

MOUNTAIN CHICKADEE* (<u>Parus</u> <u>gambeli</u>)

Common resident in coniferous forest at moderate to high elevations; also moves to deciduous woodland at lower elevations during winter.

CHESTNUT-BACKED CHICKADEE* (<u>Parus</u> <u>rufescens</u>)

Occasional to uncommon resident in dense coniferous forests of the Blue and Wallowa Mountains.

BUSHTIT (<u>Psaltriparus</u> <u>minimus</u>)   U

Hypothetical, two records: one bird seen in La Grande, Union County in October 1976; one observer. Five birds seen in La Grande, Union County on 22 May 1980; one observer.

FAMILY SITTIDAE

WHITE-BREASTED NUTHATCH* (<u>Sitta</u> <u>carolinensis</u>)

Uncommon resident of open coniferous and deciduous woodland at low to moderate elevations.

RED-BREASTED NUTHATCH* (<u>Sitta</u> <u>canadensis</u>)

Common resident in open coniferous and mixed woodland at low to high elevations; during winter also found in deciduous growth at low elevations.

PYGMY NUTHATCH* (Sitta pygmaea)

Occasional to uncommon resident. Found chiefly in ponderosa pine forest of Blue and Wallowa Mountains at moderate to high elevations.

FAMILY CERTHIIDAE

BROWN CREEPER* (Certhia familiaris)

Common resident in coniferous and mixed forest at moderate to high elevations; also moves to deciduous woods at low elevations during winter.

— Dipper —

FAMILY CINCLIDAE

DIPPER* (Cinclus mexicanus)

Common resident along swift streams in Blue and Wallowa Mountains and their higher foothills; descends to lower elevations during winter.

FAMILY TROGLODYTIDAE

HOUSE WREN* (Troglodytes aedon)

Common spring and fall migrant and summer resident. Prefers brushy habitats at low to moderate elevations.

WINTER WREN* (Troglodytes troglodytes)

Occasional to uncommon resident in dense understory of coniferous or mixed forest at low to moderate elevations; also found in deciduous growth during winter.

BEWICK'S WREN (Thyromanes bewickii)   U

Accidental, one verified record: one bird spent a week in Union, Union County during early Devember 1979. Three observers.

LONG-BILLED MARSH WREN* (Cistothorus palustris)

Locally uncommon spring and fall migrant and summer resident, occasional winter resident. Found in cattail and tule marshes at low elevations.

CANYON WREN* (Catherpes mexicanus)

Locally uncommon resident in steep arid canyon areas at low to moderate elevations. Most common along Snake and Grande Ronde Rivers in Wallowa County.

ROCK WREN* (Salpinctes obsoletus)

Common spring and fall migrant and summer resident. Less selective of habitat than Canyon Wren; rocky arid areas at low to moderate elevations preferred.

-Gray Catbird-

FAMILY MIMIDAE

GRAY CATBIRD* (<u>Dumetella</u> <u>carolinensis</u>)

Uncommon spring and fall migrant and summer resident. Found in riparian growth at low elevations; most common along Grande Ronde River in Union County.

SAGE THRASHER* (<u>Oreoscoptes</u> <u>montanus</u>)

Occasional to uncommon spring and fall migrant and summer resident in sagebrush areas of southern Union County; very rare during migration in Grande Ronde and Wallowa Valleys.

FAMILY TURDIDAE

AMERICAN ROBIN* (<u>Turdus</u> <u>migratorius</u>)

Abundant spring and fall migrant and summer resident, uncommon winter resident. Found in open and semi-open country, especially around residential areas, at low to high elevations.

VARIED THRUSH* (Ixoreus naevius)

Uncommon resident in dense coniferous forest at moderate to high elevations. Less numerous during winter when it also moves to deciduous growth at lower elevations.

HERMIT THRUSH* (Catharus guttatus)

Uncommon spring and fall migrant and summer resident, rare winter resident. Found in dense coniferous forest at moderate to high elevations; also migrates and winters in mixed and deciduous woodland at lower elevations.

SWAINSON'S THRUSH* (Catharus ustulatus)

Uncommon spring and fall migrant and summer resident in coniferous and mixed forest at moderate to high elevations. Also migrates through deciduous growth at lower elevations.

VEERY* (Catharus fuscenscens)

Common spring and fall migrant and summer resident in dense undergrowth of deciduous woodland at low elevations, usually near water.

WESTERN BLUEBIRD* (Sialia mexicana)

Uncommon spring and fall migrant and summer resident, occasional winter resident. Prefers open and lightly wooded foothill areas at low to moderate elevations.

MOUNTAIN BLUEBIRD* (Sialia currucoides)

Uncommon to common resident, irregular in winter. Prefers fields on forest edges at moderate to high elevations during summer; open foothill areas at low to moderate elevations during winter.

TOWNSEND'S SOLITAIRE* (Myadestes townsendi)

Uncommon resident. Found in open coniferous forest at moderate to high elevations during summer; open foothill country at low to moderate elevations during winter.

FAMILY SYLIVIIDAE

GOLDEN-CROWNED KINGLET* (Regulus satrapa)

Common resident. Breeds in coniferous forest at moderate to high elevations; also moves to deciduous woodland at low elevations during winter.

RUBY-CROWNED KINGLET* (Regulus calendula)

Common spring and fall migrant and summer resident, uncommon winter resident. Breeds at moderate to high elevations in coniferous forest; winters and migrates in deciduous woodland and riparian growth at low elevations.

FAMILY MOTACILLIDAE

WATER PIPIT* (Anthus spinoletta)

Common to abundant spring and fall migrant, occasional summer and winter resident. Found in open country at low elevations during migration and winter, breeds locally in alpine areas during summer.

FAMILY BOMBYCILLIDAE

BOHEMIAN WAXWING (Bombycilla garrulus)

Common to abundant winter visitor in open woodland and residential areas at low elevations; no summer records.

CEDAR WAXWING* (<u>Bombycilla</u> <u>cedrorum</u>)

Common spring and fall migrant and summer
resident, uncommon winter resident. Found in
open woodland and residential areas at low to
moderate elevations.

— Loggerhead Shrike —

FAMILY LANIIDAE

NORTHERN SHRIKE (<u>Lanius</u> <u>excubitor</u>)

Uncommon to common winter visitor in open
country or open woodland generally at low to
moderate elevations; no summer records.

LOGGERHEAD SHRIKE* (<u>Lanius</u> <u>ludovicianus</u>)

Uncommon spring and fall migrant and summer
resident, occasional winter resident. Found
in similar habitat as Northern Shrike.

FAMILY STURNIDAE

STARLING* (<u>Sturnus</u> <u>vulgaris</u>)

Abundant introduced resident in residential
areas and farmland at low to moderate
elevations.

FAMILY VIREONIDAE

SOLITARY VIREO* (Vireo solitarius)

Common spring and fall migrant and summer resident. Breeds in mixed or coniferous forest at moderate elevations; migrates through deciduous woods and riparian areas at low elevations.

RED-EYED VIREO* (Vireo olivaceus)

Uncommon spring and fall migrant and summer resident in deciduous woodland usually near water at low elevations.

WARBLING VIREO* (Vireo gilvus)

Common spring and fall migrant and summer resident in deciduous and mixed woodland and riparian areas at low to moderate elevations.

FAMILY PARULIDAE

BLACK-AND-WHITE WARBLER (Mniotilta varia) U

Accidental, one record: one adult male was heard and observed near Island City, Union County on 17 May 1980. Two observers.

TENNESSEE WARBLER (Vermivora peregrina) U

Accidental, two verified records: one bird observed at Red Bridge State Park, Union County on 27 August 1977; two observers. Two birds found in La Grande, Union County on 20-22 August 1980; two observers.

ORANGE-CROWNED WARBLER* (Vermivora celata)

Uncommon spring and fall migrant and summer resident in riparian growth and deciduous or mixed woodland with brushy understory at low to moderate elevations.

NASHVILLE WARBLER* (Vermivora ruficapilla)

Uncommon to common spring and fall migrant and summer resident. Prefers deciduous woods and brushy areas at low to moderate elevations.

YELLOW WARBLER* (Dendroica petechia)

Common, locally abundant, spring and fall migrant and summer resident. Found in deciduous or mixed woods, riparian growth, brushy areas, and residential areas usually at low elevations. Less common at moderate to high elevations.

YELLOW-RUMPED WARBLER* (Dendroica coronata)

Common spring and fall migrant and summer resident, rare winter resident. Breeds in coniferous and mixed forest at moderate elevations, migrates and winter in deciduous growth and residential areas at low elevations. The typical breeding race here is Audubon's Warbler, D. c. auduboni.

TOWNSEND'S WARBLER* (Dendroica townsendi)

Common spring and fall migrant and summer resident. Breeds in coniferous forest at moderate to high elevations, migrates at lower elevations through deciduous woods.

HERMIT WARBLER (Dendroica occidentalis)

Hypothetical: a number of records are from moderate elevations during summer in the Blue and Wallowa Mountains, but no verified sightings yet.

PALM WARBLER (<u>Dendroica</u> <u>palmarum</u>)   W

Hypothetical, one record: one bird observed at Imnaha, Wallowa County on 12 May 1978. One observer.

MAC GILLIVRAY'S WARBLER* (<u>Oporornis</u> <u>tolmiei</u>)

Uncommon spring and fall migrant and summer resident in riparian growth and other brushy areas at low to moderate elevations.

COMMON YELLOWTHROAT* (<u>Geothlypis</u> <u>trichas</u>)

Common spring and fall migrant and summer resident in marshes, lake and river borders, and wet meadows at low elevations.

YELLOW-BREASTED CHAT* (<u>Icteria</u> <u>virens</u>)

Locally uncommon summer resident in riparian growth and other brushy areas at low elevations; most common along Grande Ronde, Wallowa, and Imnaha Rivers.

WILSON'S WARBLER* (<u>Wilsonia</u> <u>pusilla</u>)

Uncommon spring and fall migrant and summer resident in deciduous woodland, riparian growth, and brushy areas at low elevations.

AMERICAN REDSTART* (<u>Setophaga</u> <u>ruticilla</u>)

Occasional spring and fall migrant and summer resident most often in riparian growth at low elevations (major river courses); breeds very locally.

FAMILY PLOCEIDAE

HOUSE SPARROW* (<u>Passer</u> <u>domesticus</u>)

Abundant introduced resident found around human settlements: cities, towns, farms, etc. at low to moderate elevations.

— Bobolink —

FAMILY ICTERIDAE

BOBOLINK* (<u>Dolichonyx</u> <u>oryzivorus</u>)

Locally uncommon spring and fall migrant and summer resident. Found in hay or unmown grass fields at low elevations.

WESTERN MEADOWLARK* (<u>Sturnella</u> <u>neglecta</u>)

Common summer resident, uncommon winter resident in open country at low to moderate elevations.

YELLOW-HEADED BLACKBIRD* (<u>Xanthocephalus</u> <u>xanthocephalus</u>)

Locally common summer resident, breeding in cattail and tule marshes usually at low elevations; forages widely as other blackbirds do.

RED-WINGED BLACKBIRD* (Agelaius phoeniceus)

Common to abundant spring and fall migrant and summer resident, uncommon winter resident. Found in open country near water at low to moderate elevations.

NORTHERN ORIOLE* (Icterus galbula)

Uncommon spring and fall migrant and summer resident. Found in deciduous woodland and groves, usually near water, at low elevations. The Bullock's Oriole, I. g. bullockii, is the rare normally occurring here.

BREWER'S BLACKBIRD* (Euphagus cyanocephalus)

Common to abundant spring and fall migrant and summer resident, uncommon winter resident. Prefers open country such as farmland, roadsides, towns, etc. at low to moderate elevations.

GREAT-TAILED GRACKLE (Quiscalus mexicanus) U

Accidental, one record: one male bird was found near Island City, Union County on 5-6 June 1980. Eight observers.

BROWN-HEADED COWBIRD* (Molothrus ater)

Common spring and fall migrant and summer resident, occasional winter resident. Found in open country, especially around cattle feed lots, at low elevations.

FAMILY THRAUPIDAE

WESTERN TANAGER* (<u>Piranga</u> <u>ludoviciana</u>)

Common spring and fall migrant and summer resident. Breeds in coniferous or mixed forest at moderate to high elevations, migrates through deciduous woods at low elevations.

FAMILY FRINGILLIDAE

ROSE-BREASTED GROSBEAK (<u>Pheucticus</u>   U
<u>ludovicianus</u>)

Hypothetical, one record: one male bird seen with Black-Headed Grosbeaks at Rhinehart near Elgin, Union County in May 1975. One observer.

BLACK-HEADED   GROSBEAK*   (<u>Pheucticus</u>
<u>melanocephalus</u>)

Common spring and fall migrant and summer resident in deciduous woodland and riparian growth at low to moderate elevations.

LAZULI BUNTING* (<u>Passerina</u> <u>amoena</u>)

Uncommon to common spring and fall migrant and summer resident. Prefers riparian growth and brushy areas at low elevations.

EVENING GROSBEAK* (<u>Hesperiphona</u> <u>vespertina</u>)

Common resident. Breeds in coniferous forest at moderate to high elevations, winters at lower elevations in deciduous or mixed woods and residential areas.

PURPLE FINCH (<u>Carpodacus</u> <u>purpureus</u>)

Very rare spring migrant in deciduous woodland and residential areas at low elevations.

CASSIN'S FINCH* (<u>Carpodacus</u> <u>cassinii</u>)

Uncommon to common resident. Breeds in
coniferous forest at moderate to high
elevations, winters at lower elevations in
coniferous or mixed woodland and irregularly
in residential areas.

HOUSE FINCH* (<u>Carpodacus</u> <u>mexicanus</u>)

Locally common resident; prefers residential
areas, farmland, and open woodland at low to
moderate elevations.

PINE GROSBEAK* (<u>Pinicola</u> <u>enucleator</u>)

Occasional to uncommon winter visitor,
occasional spring and fall migrant and summer
resident. Winters in deciduous and coniferous
woods at low to moderate elevations, breeds
in coniferous forest at moderate to high
elevations.

— Pine Grosbeak —

— Black Rosy Finch —

GRAY-CROWNED ROSY FINCH* (Leucosticte tephrocotis)

Rare to uncommon winter visitor, locally uncommon summer resident; winter status highly unpredictable and irregular. Prefers snowy open fields and hillsides at low to moderate elevations during winter; strictly an alpine bird in the Wallowa Mountains during summer.

BLACK ROSY FINCH (Leucosticte atrata)

Very rare resident in same habitat as Gray-Crowned Rosy Finch; probably breeds. Intermediate forms between the two species have been encountered.

COMMON REDPOLL (Carduelis flammea)

Rare to occasional winter visitor, highly erratic in occurrence from year to year. Found in open brushy country such as fields, farmland, and foothills at low to moderate elevations.

PINE SISKIN* (Carduelis pinus)

Common resident, irregular in occurrence in lowlands. Breeds in coniferous forest at moderate to high elevations, winters and migrates in deciduous and mixed woods and residential areas at lower elevations.

AMERICAN GOLDFINCH* (Carduelis tristus)

Common spring and fall migrant and summer resident, uncommon winter resident. Found in brushy habitats at low to moderate elevations.

RED CROSSBILL* (Loxia curvirostra)

Uncommon to common resident, wanders irregularly. Breeds in coniferous forest at moderate to high elevations, usually descends to lower elevations during winter when it is also found in deciduous woods and residential areas; may breed at any time of year.

WHITE-WINGED CROSSBILL (Loxia leucoptera)

Very rare spring and fall migrant and winter visitor to coniferous forest and woods at low to high elevations. A small flock summered near Enterprise, Wallowa County in 1977; nests were built, but no young were raised.

RUFOUS-SIDED TOWHEE* (Pipilo erythrophthalmus)

Uncommon resident in brushy areas, riparian growth, and residential areas. Found at low to moderate elevations, but most descend to lowlands during winter.

GREEN-TAILED TOWHEE (Pipilo chlorurus)

Very rare summer resident in dry foothill areas
and canyonlands at low to moderate elevations;
formerly more common. May still nest very
locally.

SAVANNAH SPARROW* (Passerculus sandwichensis)

Common spring and fall migrant and summer
resident. Found in grassy areas, agricultural
fields, and other open areas at low to moderate
elevations.

VESPER SPARROW* (Pooecetes gramineus)

Locally common spring and fall migrant and
summer resident. Prefers similar habitat as
Savannah Sparrow, but less often found around
human settlements.

LARK SPARROW* (Chondestes grammacus)

Locally uncommon spring and fall migrant and
summer resident. Found in drier fields and
sagebrush areas at low elevations.

SAGE SPARROW (Amphispiza belli)

Occasional to uncommon spring and fall migrant
and summer resident in dry grassy areas and
sagebrush flats at low elevations; may breed
in southern Union County.

DARK-EYED JUNCO* (Junco hyemalis)

Common to abundant resident. Breeds in
coniferous forest at moderate to high
elevations, winters in deciduous woodland and
residential areas at lower elevations. The
breeding race is the Oregon Junco, J. h.
oreganus, and it is also the more common form
here. The Slate-Colored Junco, J. h.
hyemalis, is a very uncommon winter visitor.

—Tree Sparrow—

TREE SPARROW (Spizella arborea)

Uncommon winter visitor, found along brushy
fence rows, hedges, and riparian growth at
low elevations.

CHIPPING SPARROW* (Spizella passerina)

Common spring and fall migrant and summer
resident. Breeds in open coniferous forest
at moderate to high elevations, migrates
through deciduous woodland and residential
areas at low elevations.

BREWER'S SPARROW* (Spizella breweri)

Uncommon spring and fall migrant and summer
resident in sagebrush and grassy areas of
southern Union County. Rare during migration
in Grande Ronde and Wallowa Valleys.

HARRIS' SPARROW (Zonotrichia querula)

Occasional winter visitor to both counties.
Most records are from brushy residential yards
and fence rows at low elevations.

WHITE-CROWNED SPARROW* (_Zonotrichia leucophrys_)

Common to abundant spring and fall migrant and summer resident, locally uncommon winter resident. Breeds on coniferous forest edges at moderate to high elevations, winters in brushy habitats and residential areas at low elevations.

GOLDEN-CROWNED SPARROW (_Zonotrichia atricapilla_)

Rare to occasional winter visitor. Found in similar habitat as Harris' Sparrow.

WHITE-THROATED SPARROW (_Zonotrichia albicollis_)   U

Hypothetical, one record: one adult bird found at feeder near Island City, Union County on 30 October 1979. One observer.

FOX SPARROW* (_Passerella iliaca_)

Uncommon spring and fall migrant and summer resident, occasional winter resident. Breeds locally on coniferous forest edges at moderate to high elevations, winters in brushy habitats and residential areas at low elevations.

LINCOLN'S SPARROW* (_Melospiza lincolnii_)

Occasional spring and fall migrant and winter visitor, rare summer resident. Found in brushy habitats at low to moderate elevations; breeds in wet highland meadows.

SONG SPARROW* (_Melospiza melodia_)

Common resident in brushy habitats, often near water, at low to moderate elevations.

LAPLAND LONGSPUR (Calcarius lapponicus)

Accidental, two records: one bird found north of Joseph, Wallowa County in November 1977; one observer. One bird found at feeder in La Grande, Union County during January 1970; two observers.

SNOW BUNTING (Plectrophenax nivalis)

Occasional to uncommon winter visitor. Found in open fields and foothill regions at low to moderate elevations.

NOTES...